PATRICIA NEWMAN

Giant Rays of Hope

Protecting **Manta Rays** to Safeguard the Sea

MILLBROOK PRESS / MINNEAPOLIS

For Narelle, Dahja, Julio, Dayra, José, Milagros, Erik, Zulema, Ana, Treysi, Jeykob, Josué, Haron, Christofer, Dulce, Camila, and Charleny—the voices of our ocean

Millbrook Press™
An imprint of Lerner Publishing Group, Inc.
241 First Avenue North
Minneapolis, MN 55401 USA

For reading levels and more information, look up this title at www.lernerbooks.com.

Illustrations on pages 10 and 28 by Laura K. Westlund.

Designed by Danielle Carnito.
Main body text set in Joanna MT Std.
Typeface provided by Monotype Typography.

Library of Congress Cataloging-in-Publication Data

Names: Newman, Patricia, 1958– author.
Title: Giant rays of hope : protecting manta rays to safeguard the sea / by Patricia Newman.
Description: Minneapolis, MN : Millbrook Press, [2025] | Includes bibliographical references and index. | Audience: Ages 9–14 | Audience: Grades 4–6 | Summary: "Kerstin Forsberg made waves in Perú when she started a community-focused project to save manta rays. Find out more about manta rays and how local people are working to save these gentle giants" —Provided by publisher.
Identifiers: LCCN 2023052821 (print) | LCCN 2023052822 (ebook) | ISBN 9798765607992 (library binding) | ISBN 9798765638569 (epub)
Subjects: LCSH: Mobulidae—Peru—Juvenile literature. | Mobulidae—Conservation—Peru—Juvenile literature.
Classification: LCC QL638.85.M6 N49 2025 (print) | LCC QL638.85.M6 (ebook) | DDC 597.3/5—dc23/eng/20240304

LC record available at https://lccn.loc.gov/2023052821
LC ebook record available at https://lccn.loc.gov/2023052822

Manufactured in the United States of America
1-1010255-51435-5/6/2024

CONTENTS

INTRODUCTION

Inventing the Future

Manta rays have the largest brains of any fish and might be able to recognize themselves in a mirror. Scientists say that manta rays are able to create mental maps of their environment, through smell and visual cues, indicating highly developed long-term memory.

Kerstin Forsberg prepares to survey Peruvian fishers for her ocean conservation work.

Off the coast of Perú, a giant manta ray silently soars through the deep blue. Her fins flap like wings as her diamond-shaped body slices through ocean swells, always feeding, always patrolling.

She shares a branch of her family tree with sharks because mantas and sharks have flexible cartilage rather than bony skeletons. And like many of her toothy cousins, she must swim constantly to stay alive. But the similarities end there. Instead of biting prey, the giant manta feeds by straining tiny animals adrift in the sea through feathery filters called gill plates.

In Spanish *manta* means "blanket," which is a fitting description because this colossus of the southern Pacific Ocean could cover not one . . . not two . . . not three . . . but four king-size beds!

As the gentle manta ray somersaults and swoops beneath the waves, danger lurks above. Humans with sharp harpoons could stab her. Poachers might kill her for her gill plates. Fishing nets might entangle and drown her. A warming ocean affects her food supply. These dangers place her entire species at serious risk of extinction.

But there is hope.

Kerstin Forsberg has challenged herself to convince the fishers of Perú that giant manta rays are not the catch of the day but are, instead, critical to the future of their fishing communities. Despite generations of accumulated knowledge about the best places to fish, the rhythms of the tides, and seasonal weather patterns, fishers were unaware of their own effect on nature. Many of them believed the ocean held an unlimited supply of fish and did not understand why the number and the size of the fish in their nets decreased every year. They didn't know that the world's fishing industry tends to catch too many fish at once so the fish cannot breed fast enough to recover, and without these fish, ocean habitats become unbalanced. They didn't know the manta rays and turtles accidentally captured in their nets worsened this overfishing. And they didn't know human-caused climate change, pollution, and habitat loss make fish survival even more uncertain.

In a lucky twist of fate, manta ray scientist Andrea Marshall gave Kerstin the ideal way to make her goal a reality. Although Kerstin knew Andrea tagged mantas with satellite tracking devices to study where and how far they traveled, the two ocean lovers had never met. "A giant manta ray that she'd tagged was swimming between Ecuador and Perú," Kerstin recalls. "But the tag had stopped transmitting in northern Perú—on land, not in the sea, which was weird." Andrea needed to find it to collect the data on it.

"I was intrigued," Kerstin says. "Where would it be, this small device in the middle of an entire coastal region? It was like finding a needle in a haystack." She posted flyers in the fishing villages of northern Perú and asked local volunteers to spread the word. Andrea also offered a reward to persuade people to help.

Then they waited. A few days later, a fisher from northern Perú called Kerstin. He had found Andrea's tag. "We were utterly delighted," Andrea said. "It was the first definitive information that mantas were moving between Ecuador and Perú."

"[Mantas are] so large, but at the same time so elegant," Kerstin says. Their uniqueness made her want to find out more about them. Why do mantas visit the waters of Perú? How do we identify them? Why don't we know more about them? Could learning to protect mantas help fishers protect the ocean and ensure a lifetime of good catches?

"[Mantas are] so large, but at the same time so elegant."
—Kerstin Forsberg

Andrea Marshall tags a giant manta ray off the coast of Ecuador. She inserts the tag between the manta's pectoral fin and body where it won't interfere with swimming or harm any of the manta's internal organs. The tag will transmit the manta's location and depth.

GENTLE GIANTS

Dorsal View

- Known by the scientific name *Mobula birostris*
- Between 13 to 30 feet (4 to 9 m) from one pectoral (side) wingtip to the other
- Females larger than males
- Diamond body shape ideal for swimming
- Large size to protect against predators
- Eyes on the side of their head
- Weigh up to 4,400 pounds (2,000 kg)
- Must swim to survive
- Largest brain of all fish
- One beat of the winglike fins able to propel them 20 miles (32 km) per hour
- White shoulder patches shaped like right triangles make a black T
- Leap out of the water to feed, communicate with other mantas, clean themselves, play, evade predators, or even control their body temperature

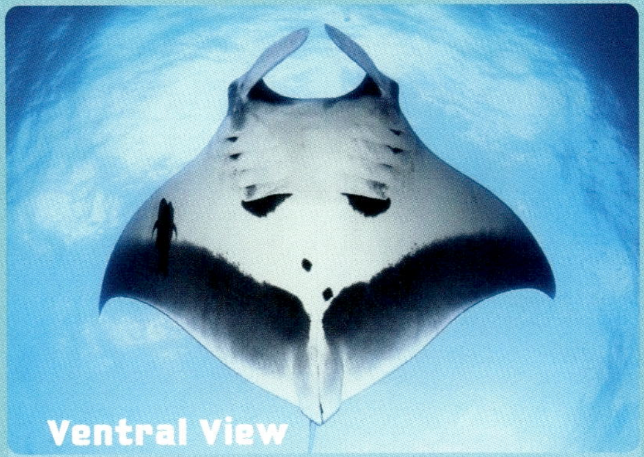

Ventral View

- Spots usually clustered near the bottom of their bellies
- Back edge of the pectoral fins usually shaded black
- A unique pattern of spots on each individual, making it easier to identify them
- Are able to reproduce at about eight to ten years of age
- Hatch from soft eggs inside mother's uterus and feed on milk before birth
- One to two pups born to females every two to five years

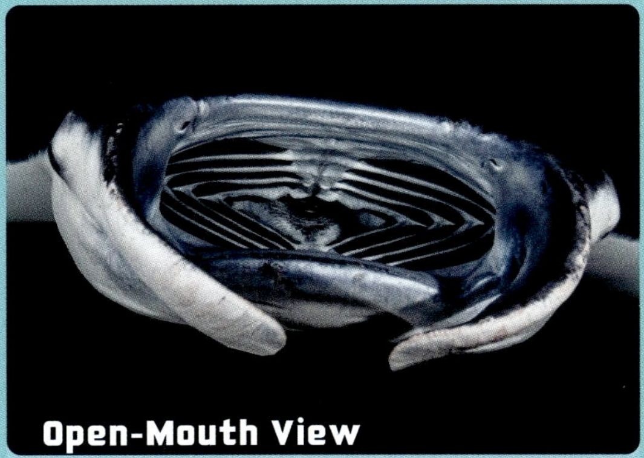

Open-Mouth View

- Spend their time in the open ocean
- Suck gallons of seawater into their mouths to feed on zooplankton
- Zooplankton strained out by feathery gill plates
- Usually remain near the surface during the day
- Dive down to 164 feet (50 m) to feed at night but resurface every few minutes, possibly to stay warm
- Cephalic fins on either side of the mouth; usually black on the inside

CHAPTER 1

Making Waves

Kerstin loved the ocean from an early age. As a toddler, she plays on the beach in Ancón, Perú, near Lima.

Kerstin began laying the foundation for conservation in Perú long before Andrea's lost manta ray tag.

When Kerstin was eight years old, she was lucky enough to have a tiny zoo on her elementary school campus on the outskirts of Lima. The zoo was meant to bring students closer to nature. Kerstin loved the monkeys, penguins, and ocelots, but her classmates mostly ignored them. Their lack of interest made Kerstin sad so she created a club called Friends of the School's Zoo. Club members created signs for their classmates and parents with facts about each critter and why it was important to Perú.

Kerstin locates a stranded turtle on a beach in Perú.

Her love of animals inspired her to study biology at Universidad Nacional Agraría La Molina in Lima. During her last year in college, Kerstin went to Brasil for an internship at a sea turtle conservation program. She learned that sea turtles have helped keep the ocean

KYOSHA, THE LITTLE WHALE OF PEACE

When Kerstin was ten years old, a captive orca at the Vancouver Aquarium in Canada inspired her to write a conservation story that was published in the *Apple Magazine*.

In Kerstin's story, Kyosha the orca lived in the Pacific Ocean on the coast of Perú. An oil spill from a factory polluted the water, and Kyosha became sick. Humans rescued her and took her to an aquarium to heal.

"The good people who had taken [Kyosha] in were also dedicated to teaching the children how important it is to take care of the water. They were taught that contamination not only made animals sick but also humans," Kerstin wrote.

She ended her story with Kyosha's thoughts, *"I know that these children are going to be much more responsible with the world around them when they grow up. Because they are teaching them from childhood to learn to take care of tomorrow's world."*

Kerstin is still teaching children to take care of tomorrow's world.

healthy for about one hundred million years. They eat a variety of algae, tiny marine animals, and fish, which helps balance the food web and carry nutrients from the open ocean to beaches and coastal sand dunes.

After her internship in Brasil, Kerstin returned to school and designed a class project to study sea turtles in her own country. She chose the village of Zorritos in the Tumbes region of northern Perú because many dead sea turtles washed ashore there. As she patrolled the beaches looking for dead or injured turtles, she counted them, measured them, and recorded their species to investigate the extent of the problem. But then her class ended—and so did her project. Kerstin graduated and found a job advising business leaders interested in eco-friendly strategies. But the sea turtles stayed on her mind.

STEPPING UP

"I wanted to do more," Kerstin says. After graduation, she applied for and received a grant to continue studying the problem. "At that time, I felt proud because this was my first grant. I was competing [against people] with Ph.D.s, and I was this twenty-two-year-old kid."

Kerstin worked with youth to count the number of dead sea turtles on the beach. She spoke to fishers about the number of times turtles became entangled in their nets. And she worked with teachers to create

The fishers of Tumbes come to Puerto Pizarro to sell their catch.

sea turtle lessons to share with students—children who one day might become Perú's future fishers.

During the project, Kerstin built connections with professors, teachers, students, fishers, and leaders in Tumbes. "Our study soon became a community platform," she says. "We had more than one hundred [young volunteers], and I was struck by the interest [in people wanting to join us]."

Kerstin's unexpected success made her stop and think about her full-time job. While it felt useful, was it as important as developing and leading her own environmental projects? Her sea turtle project had only scratched the surface of the disconnect between many Zorritos fishers and their struggle to make a living with fewer fish in the sea, smaller fish in their nets, and polluted rivers and beaches.

KERSTIN'S TURTLES

When Kerstin first designed her sea turtle project, turtles were caught for profit. Fishers hunted them for their meat. Turtles died entangled in fishing nets. And their shells were used as decorations in homes and businesses. The data Kerstin had gathered about the number of dead sea turtles, their size, and their species was a start, but it wasn't a solution to the problem.

The grant she received made all the difference. The money allowed Kerstin to travel twenty hours by bus from Lima to the village of Zorritos every month. She recruited student volunteers from the Universidad Nacional de Tumbes (National University of Tumbes) and trained them—many the children of fishers—to photograph, measure, and identify the species of turtles they found on the beach. In one year, Kerstin and her volunteers recorded 260 stranded sea turtles from four species: green, olive ridley, hawksbill, and leatherback.

Kerstin also taught local fishers about the importance of sea turtle conservation, and many agreed to help with her project. When a turtle swam into their nets, the fishers identified its species, weighed it, and measured it. They gave injured turtles basic first aid. Then the fishers reported where they found the turtle and where they released it back into the wild.

Schoolchildren joined the effort to save sea turtles. Ana Tello, aged nine, visited hotels and restaurants in Zorritos with her classmates. The children persuaded business owners to remove turtle shell decorations because displaying the shells as art encouraged sea turtle hunting. The owners who agreed received special turtle protection postcards designed by the children. Years later when the students were in high school, some of them returned to these hotels and restaurants. They did not see any turtle shells. "We changed our way of thinking and our culture," Ana says. "I was part of that change."

These fishers measure a sea turtle to gather information for Kerstin's project.

***Right*: Ana Tello**
***Below*: A winning postcard design by Anyelo Farias Serna.**

"I [was] not reaching my full potential," Kerstin says. So she took a leap of faith. She quit her job to follow a path with no clear direction and no guaranteed income. Her parents understood. Her friends thought she was foolish. But Kerstin believed in herself.

Two years before the manta tag went missing, Kerstin created Planeta Océano (Planet Ocean) to change the way conservation works in coastal Perú. In the past, activists would launch projects to save a single species, hoping the community would eventually follow along. The projects focused on saving nature because it was beautiful, rather than emphasizing how humans benefit from it. But Kerstin wanted to change that model and began with local people by giving them starring roles in their own conservation story.

Children learn about the ocean by playing games that Kerstin invented.

STAR POWER

Kerstin returned to Zorritos, a community that already trusted her. She knew Planeta Océano needed to show the community how we are all connected to the sea. The ocean provides about half of the oxygen on our planet and much of our food. Even our drinking water begins with the ocean. The sun's rays cause surface water to evaporate as water vapor and condense into clouds. Water drops form inside the clouds and eventually fall as rain, sleet, snow, or hail. "We all have the duty and responsibility to take care of life on this planet," Kerstin says. "No matter how far we live from the ocean . . . [we] cannot disconnect from it."

"No matter how far we live from the ocean . . . [we] cannot disconnect from it."
—Kerstin Forsberg

Perú's mangrove forests help keep the ocean healthy, but pollution from local shrimp farms puts these important trees at risk.

José Zapata

Kerstin and her Planeta Océano team started with schools. They asked teachers how they taught ocean science in their classrooms. Surprisingly, they didn't! Children and teens who lived only steps from the beach, played on the warm sand, felt cool sea breezes on their skin, and tasted the salty tang in the air never studied the ocean in school. So Kerstin showed teachers how to teach ocean concepts using art, experiments, games, and seaside field trips. Together they established the Marine Educators Network of Northern Perú to improve ocean education and share new lessons with thirty-five hundred other teachers and the fifteen thousand students they taught.

Kerstin also hosted after-school youth workshops to help groups of young conservationists identify environmental problems in their own communities and figure out how to solve them. "You don't need to be a Ph.D. researcher to help with science," she says.

Thirteen-year-old José Zapata and his group worked with scientists to study how a shrimp farm affected a mangrove forest between Perú and Ecuador. They learned how mangrove trees grow in estuaries where seawater and fresh water mix. These trees protect the coastline during storms, collect and store carbon pollution from the air, and provide a protected place for young fish to grow up. "We discovered bacteria from a nearby shrimp farm in the water," José says. "It was killing the mangroves."

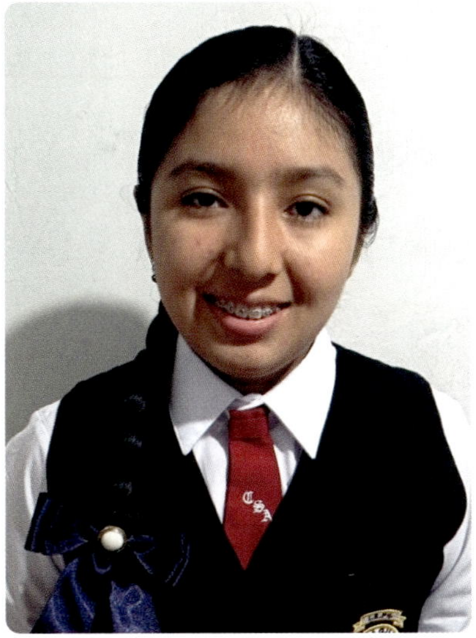

Milagros Quispe Espinosa

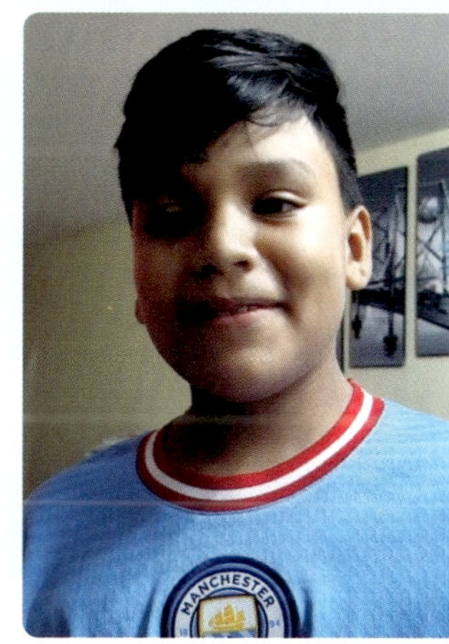

Julio Suárez (*right*) and his classmates measure and record fish sizes in Puerto Pizarro's busy fish market (*above*).

While José concentrated on mangroves, fourteen-year-old Milagros Quispe Espinosa and her group focused on educating the people of Tumbes about the shrimp farm's pollution. "We gave [community] workshops about how the shrimp farm polluted the marsh and how it affected the animals and plants that lived there," she says. Milagros and her team then invited the community to brainstorm possible solutions.

Twelve-year-olds Dahja Castañeda and Julio Suárez and thirteen-year-old Dayra Juarez visited Puerto Pizarro in the Tumbes region. As the port bustled with fishers bringing in their daily catch, the students observed the fish market. They recorded the different species of fish for sale and measured them to see if they were within the government's minimum size limits. Fish smaller than the limit should be returned to the sea because a healthy ocean needs young fish to grow up and reproduce. Dahja, Julio, and Dayra created a presentation and a game to share with their entire school about the importance of fish sizes and the dangers of overfishing.

WHAT DOES THE OCEAN MEAN TO YOU?

"I am a firm believer that youth and children are not just the future, but rather the present," Kerstin says. "They can contribute starting from now." Five young people who have worked with Planeta Océano share how they feel about the ocean:

Dayra Juarez, aged thirteen, says, **"The ocean is more than what I see in front of me. It is all around the world. It is a mystery of many things waiting to be discovered."**

Narelle Casabonne Forsberg, aged nine, says, **"I've always been close to the ocean. I'm always there when my mom teaches other kids about the ocean. Every time I see the ocean, it's like magic, light, and happiness."**

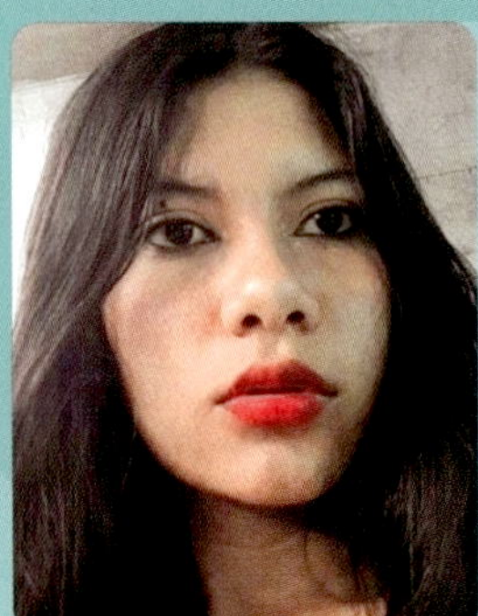

Treysi Calderón, aged sixteen, says, **"I want to create an organization like Planeta Océano to pass on what I have learned about taking care of the sea."**

Dahja Castañeda, aged twelve, says, **"The ocean is the source of life, and I am part of that life. It is my mission to take care of it."**

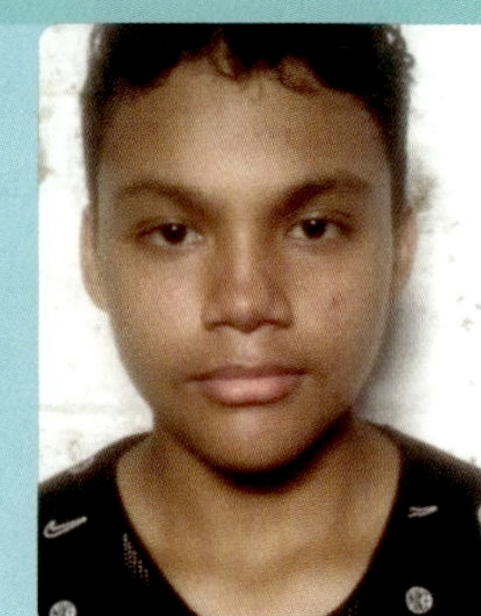

Jeykob García, aged fourteen, says, **"It's difficult to think how big and deep the ocean is. The fact we've only explored about 10 percent of it says it all."**

Julio also learned that every time he littered, the trash would eventually flow out to sea because all pollution becomes ocean pollution. "The fish eat the trash. And then I eat the fish. I was eating my own rubbish!" he says. "Planeta Océano changed the way I think."

"The students lead by example," says Martin Dioses, a member of the Marine Educators Network. "And their parents follow their lead." Adults with no formal ocean education learned to celebrate their connection to the sea.

Waves of change flowed throughout the Tumbes region as kids, teens, and teachers empowered by Planeta Océano spoke up on behalf of their communities. By 2011 the community was primed for the next challenge. Enter Andrea Marshall and her lost manta tag.

"Planeta Océano changed the way I think."
—Julio Suárez

MANTA MUSINGS

Andrea's call for help made Kerstin wonder: Why didn't she see manta rays in modern Peruvian art, clothing, movies, or ads? Did fishers encounter them? Had mantas ever been part of Peruvian culture?

Kerstin found out that the ancient Moche civilization decorated their pottery with many ocean images, including rays. These images provide clues about their importance to the people. The Moche thrived in Perú's coastal and inland valleys (100 to 800 CE) and considered the ocean a sacred place. They fished for many kinds of rays and perhaps even

Museo Larco, Lima - Perú ML003234

The Moche poured superheated terra-cotta into molds and fired them in kilns to make pottery. Artists carved the faces of priests, warriors, fishers, and musicians into the molds to share stories and scenes from daily life.

had spiritual visions involving these graceful swimmers. Although manta rays disappeared from art when the ancient Moche civilization died out, they have resurfaced in the experiments of present-day scientists.

Mantas slip through the ocean scooping up plankton in their cavernous mouths. As they swim between the surface and the ocean depths, they carry surface nutrients deep underwater and deepwater nutrients to the surface. Healthy mantas signal a healthy ocean with an abundant food supply. Scientists believe the waters off the coast of Ecuador and Perú have about twenty-two thousand giant manta rays, the largest population in the world. And they are protected by Ecuador's government. But if the mantas swim south to the waters of Perú, no such protection exists.

Why has Perú forgotten about these magnificent creatures? Threads of an idea began to stitch together in Kerstin's mind. Could giant manta rays be the key to helping fishers see the ocean as something to protect rather than something to take advantage of? Her instincts said yes, but how?

Arresting and mysterious, this all-black giant manta ray cruises through the ocean. Scientists describe it as melanistic because it has a higher than typical amount of black coloring.

WHAT'S A FLAGSHIP SPECIES?

Giant pandas, Bengal tigers, bald eagles, African elephants, and mountain gorillas are all flagship species. People marvel at the way they look or the way they behave. Flagship species help conservation organizations grab people's attention and make them care about protecting the environment.

Giant manta rays are the flagship of Kerstin's work. This iconic species acts as a symbol for the problems fishers and ocean creatures face in the waters off the coast of Perú. "We have to protect the manta rays, but in order to protect them, we also have to protect everything around [them]," Kerstin says.

CHAPTER 2

Embracing Manta Rays

When people swim with manta rays, they learn to respect the gentle giants.

Kerstin decided to introduce giant manta rays to the people of Tumbes before convincing them to help protect mantas. Team Planeta Océano asked fishers to alert them whenever they spotted a manta. The fishers treated it as a challenge: Who could spot the next giant manta?

Villagers boarded boats with Kerstin and her team and motored offshore to search for manta rays. Kerstin and her team taught the villagers how to swim with mantas, as scuba divers did, to experience their size and gracefulness. "It was like a spaceship was floating over me in the middle of the sea," says Ricardo Sanjinez, one of the university students who'd also volunteered for Kerstin's sea turtle project.

Ten-year-olds Andy and Jorge swam with mantas too. At first, they were afraid, but after watching a giant manta swim around them they agreed it was the best experience of their lives. They told all their friends about the manta and began painting murals in their village to share manta ray magic.

Planeta Océano and the Marine Educators Network developed manta ray lessons for the classroom. Students learned about their size, their diet, their habits, and the important clues they gave scientists about the health of the ocean. Manta costume contests

Team members at Planeta Océano share their enthusiasm for giant manta rays with local children.

Jorge Andrés Zapata paints a manta mural in Tumbes.

and parades increased the community's awareness of these magnificent creatures.

Kerstin also worked with other conservation organizations to count the number of manta landings, or the times fishers brought dead mantas ashore. In one year, Planeta Océano volunteers counted more than ten manta landings—and some of these mantas were pregnant. While ten fish may not sound like a lot, female manta rays breed only every two to five years, and females are pregnant for at least a year before giving birth to one to two pups. Because giant manta rays' reproduction rate is so low, losing even a few can seriously affect their population.

Scientists estimate that in the last seventy-five years, half to three-quarters of the entire manta population has died from overfishing. Kerstin feared the mantas of Perú would either become entangled in fishers' nets as bycatch or be poached by the ever-growing gill plate trade, which has not yet reached Perú but might one day soon.

A joyful celebration of manta rays

"It was like a spaceship was floating over me in the middle of the sea."
—Ricardo Sanjinez

DOUBLE TROUBLE

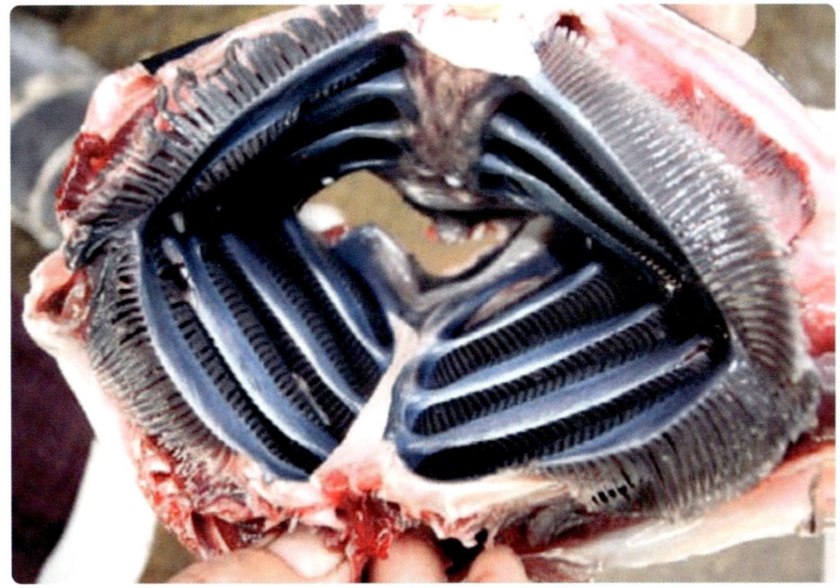
Poachers kill manta rays for their gill plates, which they dry and sell in Asian markets.

Just as poachers hunt rhinos for their horns, elephants for their ivory tusks, and pangolins for their scales, some people catch giant manta rays for their gill plates. Fishers harpoon or net mantas and sell them to buyers in China for $40 to $500 each. The gill plate trade claims that simmering manta ray gill plates in a "health tonic soup" is an ancient Chinese treatment to boost the immune system and help treat chicken pox in children. But the first reference to the "benefits" of gill plates in traditional Chinese medicine occurs in 1976, not ancient times. The gill plate trade also claims manta gill plates reduce inflammation and help with blood circulation and breastfeeding, even though no medical evidence exists to support these claims. In reality, manta gill plates are loaded with mercury, arsenic, cadmium, and lead—poisonous heavy metals filtered from the ocean and linked to developmental problems in children, as well as cancer and kidney disease in children and adults. Scientists believe the phony medical claims are nothing more than a clever marketing ploy to boost the gill plate traders' profits.

Kerstin needed to protect Perú's manta rays *before* the poachers arrived. And she hoped this protection might also eventually include entanglement, or bycatch. Entanglement isn't as sinister as the gill plate trade, but it is even more common.

To start, Kerstin reached out to some local fishers to learn more about what happens when mantas are caught in their nets. Jesús Yovera, a Tumbes fisher for more than twenty years, loads his net in his boat at five thirty each morning, motors several miles offshore, and casts his net in the water. By quarter after seven, he raises his net filled with fish and an occasional manta ray.

MEET THE MOBULIDS

The giant manta ray is one member of a group of rays called mobulids.

Oceanic manta ray (also called giant manta ray)

- Scientific name: *Mobula birostris*
- Weight: Up to 4,400 pounds (2,000 kg)
- Life span: About forty years
- Distribution: Tropical waters around the world as far north as New Jersey and as far south as Australia, including Perú
- Status: Endangered

Reef manta ray

- Scientific name: *Mobula alfredi*
- Weight: 1,500 pounds (680 kg)
- Life span: About forty years
- Distribution: Western Pacific Ocean from Japan to Australia, the Indian Ocean from India and Indonesia to South Africa, and the Red Sea
- Status: Vulnerable

Reef manta rays

Caribbean manta ray

- Scientific name: *Mobula cf. birostris*
- Weight: Up to 2,200 pounds (1,000 kg)
- Life span: About forty years
- Distribution: Caribbean Sea and Gulf of Mexico
- Status: Not listed; not yet an officially recognized species of manta ray

Longhorned pygmy devil ray

- Scientific name: *Mobula eregoodootenkee*
- Weight: Up to 55 pounds (25 kg)
- Life span: Unknown
- Distribution: From South Africa and the Red Sea and the Arabian Sea to Australia, Papua New Guinea, and Taiwan
- Status: Endangered

West Atlantic pygmy devil ray

- Scientific name: *Mobula hypostoma*
- Weight: Likely up to 55 pounds (25 kg)
- Life span: Unknown
- Distribution: Coastal waters of the western Atlantic from North Carolina to the Gulf of Mexico, the Caribbean, and Argentina
- Status: Endangered

Shorthorned pygmy devil ray

- Scientific name: *Mobula kuhlii*
- Weight: Up to 55 pounds (25 kg)
- Life span: Unknown
- Distribution: From the eastern coast of South Africa, the Red Sea, and the Arabian Sea to Indonesia and northeast Australia
- Status: Endangered

Spinetail devil ray

- Scientific name: *Mobula mobular*
- Weight: Up to 661 pounds (300 kg)
- Life span: About fifteen years
- Distribution: Around the world in the warm waters of the Mediterranean and Caribbean Seas, the Gulf of Mexico, the Red Sea, the Arabian Gulf, and off the coast of Perú
- Status: Endangered

Spinetail devil rays

Munk's pygmy devil ray

- Scientific name: *Mobula munkiana*
- Weight: Up to 55 pounds (25 kg)
- Life span: Unknown
- Distribution: From México's Sea of Cortez to the Galápagos Islands and the coast of Perú
- Status: Vulnerable

Munk's pygmy devil rays

East Atlantic pygmy devil ray

- Scientific name: *Mobula rochebrunei*
- Weight: Up to 66 pounds (30 kg)
- Life span: Unknown
- Distribution: Waters of West Africa
- Status: Endangered

Sicklefin devil ray

- Scientific name: *Mobula tarapacana*
- Weight: Up to 882 pounds (400 kg)
- Life span: About fifteen years
- Distribution: All tropical oceans, including the waters of Perú
- Status: Endangered

Bentfin devil ray

- Scientific name: *Mobula thurstoni*
- Weight: Up to 440 pounds (200 kg)
- Life span: Unknown but at least ten years
- Distribution: All tropical oceans, including the waters of Perú
- Status: Endangered

The mantas cause trouble for Jesús because they are heavy and tear his net, which he must pay to fix. Jesús and his fellow fishers do not make a lot of money and often live in poverty. They are called small-scale, or artisanal, fishers because they fish with small boats, a relatively small net, and basically no fish-finding technology. They've learned the hard way that hauling a 1,500-pound (680 kg) manta back to shore is usually not worth it. Manta ray bycatch is a lose-lose situation for both mantas and fishers.

TACKLING PROBLEMS

But simply *telling* Jesús to save manta rays wouldn't work. Why should he change the proven fishing practices he had learned from his parents and grandparents? He braves icy winds, rolling waves, and drenching downpours, his weathered face evidence of his years at sea. Didn't Jesús know more about fishing than Kerstin?

So she tried to understand his work by asking questions about the problems he faced, the habitats he crossed, and the species he saw to convince him to help the ocean by saving mantas. Kerstin interviewed other fishers and patterns began to emerge. The Zorritos fishers said they struggled with smaller catches each year—both in the size of the fish and the number of fish in their nets. And bycatch was

"We are not activists. We are engagers."
—Kerstin Forsberg

Meeting fishers and listening to their stories improves Planeta Océano's conservation work.

damaging their equipment. "From your point of view, what can we do to [keep the mantas from getting] accidentally stuck?" she asked each of them. They suggested reporting mantas sightings in real time, placing one person in charge at every port to dive and untangle manta rays from nets, and reimbursing fishers who cut their nets to free mantas.

Listening was an important part of these brainstorming sessions. Kerstin had no intention of forcing change on the fishing community, and she certainly did not expect these small-scale fishers to stop fishing. Instead, Kerstin wanted to help them fish sustainably by understanding ocean science and respecting fish size limits so the ocean could continue to produce food for other fish and us. "We are not activists. We are engagers," she says of Planeta Océano. They approach fishers and ask what problems they are facing, which Kerstin says leads to "a sense of ownership because people really want to feel part of this change."

After interviewing the fishers, Kerstin and her team put the next step of their plan into action. In 2013 they drafted a national manta protection policy to make manta hunting illegal and submitted it to the Peruvian government. Then they waited, planning the ways they would celebrate this conservation milestone.

The Marine Educators Network trains teachers to become ocean educators so they can share the knowledge with their students.

But days passed with no word from the government. Then weeks. Then months. The silence was deafening.

Kerstin persevered. She took the government's silence to mean *not now* instead of *no*. Planeta Océano continued to learn more about giant manta rays and to excite the community about these acrobatic swimmers with school programs, manta parades, and manta counts.

AN OCEAN SECRET

The southern Pacific Ocean along the coast of Perú is the most productive marine environment on the planet where marine life of all kinds meet and mingle. The secret to this abundance is the motion of the ocean—specifically its currents.

An equatorial current travels east along the equator from the Galápagos Islands conveying warm water and a huge array of marine life (including giant manta rays) to the northern coast of Perú.

The Humboldt Current begins in the Southern Ocean near Antarctica and flows north delivering cold oxygen-rich water to the Pacific Ocean along Perú's central and southern coastline.

A process called upwelling occurs here, where coastal winds push warmer surface water out to sea creating space for deep cold water to rise. The cold water carries nutrients that fertilize the surface. And *bam!* Masses of oxygen-making plants called phytoplankton and tiny zooplankton grow. They lure fish of every size and description to take advantage of the abundant food supply. Scientists estimate that the upwelling supports about 20 percent of fish caught around the world.

So protecting this region is critical. Planeta Océano combines marine science with traditional fishing knowledge to help the people of Perú understand another secret: healthy mantas mean a healthy ocean.

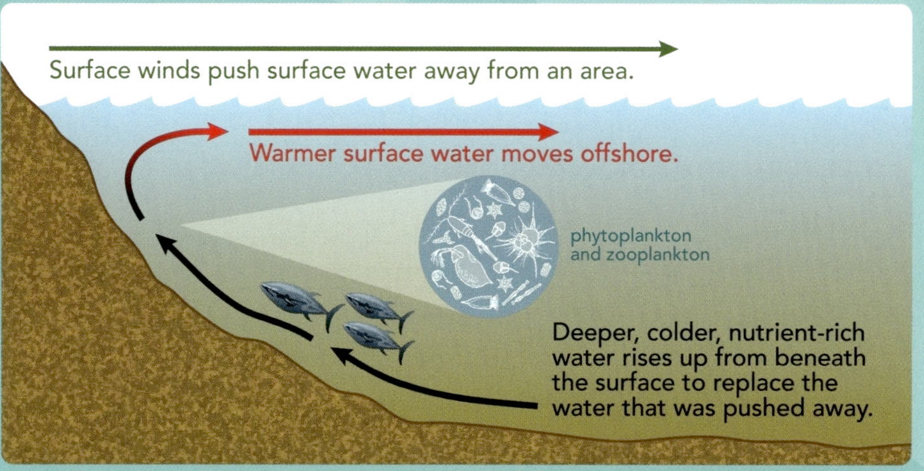

Wind blows warmer surface water away from the shore, leaving space for colder, nutrient-rich water to rise up from the deep (*above*). The nutrients in the deep water support an abundance of microscopic life, which feeds larger animals, including this shoal of grunt fish (*below*) and manta rays.

Planeta Océano also started an identification database to track the specific mantas that visit the waters of Perú and how often they return. Volunteers taught divers and fishers to take a photo of a manta's white ventral side (belly). The markings are as unique to each manta as our fingerprints are to us. Photographing a giant manta ray takes practice. The water is somewhat murky because of all the plankton in the sea. And mantas cruise the open water at a speedy 20 miles (32 km) per hour. Photographers must either be in the perfect position as a giant manta glides over them, or they must swim super fast to catch up. Despite these challenges, the new database had more than thirty photos when this book was published.

Then the unexpected happened.

On a warm April morning in 2015, some fishers thrust giant manta rays—and Kerstin—into the spotlight.

Every giant manta ray has unique markings on its belly.

CHAPTER 3

From Hunters to Ambassadors

Mantas soar freely through the water, unless they run into a fishing net.

"It was a fishing day like any other," Erik Cruz recalls. Around midnight, Erik; his father, Edgardo Cruz; and one other crew member hauled in a good catch. They decided to secure their net, toss the anchor overboard, and sleep for a few hours before fishing again at four in the morning. The dark and peaceful sea gently rocked them to sleep.

A couple of hours later, Erik startled awake as the boat violently careened this way and that. "It was totally dark," he recalls. "It was terrifying!"

Something big was tangled in the anchor line. Was it a whale? Whales can sink small fishing boats. Every time the creature tried to dive, it threatened to break the boat into pieces. "Cut the rope! We're going down," Edgardo yelled. But all they had was a small fishing knife—too small to quickly cut the heavy anchor line. The other crew member, risking the boat and their lives, called the port to see how much money they could get for this catch.

Kerstin with Edgardo Cruz, the fisher who changed everything

As they struggled to keep the creature near the surface and keep the boat from sinking, they argued. Should they protect their boat and saw through the anchor line or risk everything to haul in what must be a monster? Back and forth they went, salty language flying. Finally, they decided to reel it in—slowly, slowly—and secure it to the back of the boat.

"We knew it was big," Edgardo says. "We didn't know it was huge!" And it wasn't a whale but the biggest manta ray they had ever seen: a 1.5 ton (1.4 t) giant. They figured a manta this large must be worth something.

Edgardo and his crew towed the manta ray behind their boat, their small diesel engine straining. What should have been a two-hour ride back to shore took six hours. At some point during the struggle, the manta died.

When they reached the port, Erik hopped out of his father's boat into shallow water. With the help of twenty other fishers, he floated the manta ray to the beach. A bystander offered his tow truck to haul it ashore. The fishers spent hours bringing the manta home and expected to earn a lot of money. But giant manta ray meat is not popular in restaurants. If a manta is entangled in a net, it might be eaten, but it's not highly sought after. So despite its size, Edgardo and his crew only earned about eighty-one dollars for their efforts.

As the dead manta hung suspended in midair, spectators recorded the event from every angle. The photos went viral. The media called the manta ray a "monster." Others labeled Edgardo a villain for not releasing the animal. But he had only been trying to feed his family. He locked himself in his house, turned off his cell phone, refused to speak with anyone, and wore a disguise if he had to leave his house.

The manta ray Edgardo caught was the largest he had ever seen.

When Kerstin heard about the manta ray, she saw her chance to correct the spread of false information by ignorant newscasters. "I remember the frustration I felt at that moment," she says. "The local reporter made fun of the manta and said it's a monster, it's rare in Perú. It's dangerous." Kerstin appeared on several news shows to share the truth about these gentle giants and the hardships the artisanal fishing community faced. Then she said something that made everyone take notice: manta rays are worth more to Perú alive than dead. Kerstin always closed her interviews with an invitation to government ministers to contact her about the manta protection legislation Planeta Océano had proposed two years ago.

A government official called Kerstin the next day! Eight months after Edgardo's fateful catch, Perú finally passed a resolution that made it illegal to catch manta rays on purpose.

But legal protection was only the beginning.

TRANSFORMATIONS

Kerstin had started Planeta Océano to place "people at the center . . . of conservation." She calls them "the prime actors and stars of this conservation work." Edgardo and his colossal manta ray provided a unique opportunity. Kerstin invited him to be a manta ambassador and lead boat tours for travelers in his spare time. To recruit additional fishers, the Planeta Océano team posted banners around the Tumbes region and the neighboring Piura district that said, "Learn more about how mantas are worth more alive than dead." The ecotours would not only support the conservation of Perú's wondrous manta rays, but they would also demonstrate the importance of protecting our ocean.

TROUBLED WATERS

Manta rays sail effortlessly beneath the waves as if they don't have a care in the world, but a deeper dive reveals trouble brewing.

Our climate is changing as record levels of carbon dioxide from fossil fuels pollute the atmosphere and warm the ocean. Because of warming temperatures, scientists predict tropical waters such as those off the coast of northern Perú may lose up to one-half of the zooplankton they normally produce. What will happen to mantas with only half of their food supply?

They also face the danger of plastic pollution. Most of the plastic in the ocean is about the size of your pinkie fingernail or smaller, which means manta rays can easily scoop it up as they feed. Scientists have found evidence of plastics in manta ray poop and vomit. Will the chemicals in plastic interfere with the health and reproduction of manta rays?

Oil and mining companies pose additional threats. They are lobbying governments around the world for permission to drill for oil and dig into the seafloor for minerals to make smartphones and computers, but at what cost to manta rays? Mining operations could destroy marine habitats and interfere with the feeding and reproductive habits of mantas and other marine animals.

Taken individually, these threats are serious. Together they make Kerstin's job as manta protector even tougher—and more important.

Manta rays face threats from tiny, floating plastic pieces that look like food (*above*) and oil rigs that can destroy marine habitats (*below*).

"It's not enough to just research or educate," Kerstin says. "You need to think about creative solutions that can support the livelihoods of these impoverished communities."

In their first meeting, Team Planeta Océano asked the fishers what they knew about manta rays and how much they earned fishing. Kerstin wanted to gauge their interest in using their fishing boats to bring tourists to see the mantas. Some fishers dropped out, but many others, including Edgardo, remained. He became a founding partner in an organization called the Asociación Ecoturística de Pescadores Manta Pacífico Tropical (Tropical Pacific Manta Fishers Ecotourism Association). The fishers received the necessary education to build an ecotourism business from a grant awarded to Planeta Océano. After decades on the water, the fishers already understood ocean dynamics and the rhythms of marine life. So, Kerstin and her team added scientific knowledge to their storehouse of information, including data about the Humboldt Current and equatorial current and how the ocean supports life on land. Another class focused on the latest manta ray science, behavior, and conservation, so the fishers could share this information with their passengers.

But Kerstin and her team didn't stop there.

Fishers could apply to Planeta Océano for small loans to repair and equip their boats. Tour boats would need life jackets, snorkels, masks, and places for tourists to sit. In the tourism business, tour operators must keep customers happy if they want glowing word-of-mouth reviews or five-star online ratings. English classes helped fishers talk to international travelers. Planeta Océano also offered classes on safety and managing a small business, provided financial assistance when needed, and completed the official paperwork to register the boats as tourist vessels.

Edgardo welcomed engineers from Lima and biologists from other countries aboard his boat, *Pollito*. "I was shy in the beginning," he says. But passengers asked *him* questions. *He* was the source of knowledge.

"You need to think about creative solutions."
—Kerstin Forsberg

Kerstin prepares to swim with mantas on an early ecotourism trip.

"Every trip I learned something different that stayed with me and my family," he says. His confidence grew. "Before my only goal was fish-kill-sell. Now I fish-conserve-preserve. My learning and teaching will stay after my death."

If you book a tour on Edgardo's boat, you might get your first peek at a manta ray basking just beneath the surface of the water. Perhaps the tip of its broad wing breaks through the waves before slowly curving away as the manta dives. You might slip into the water, breathing through a snorkel, and tingle with anticipation as a dark shape rises out of the deep. Perhaps the ray would swim under you, belly up, soaring with ease.

You would become a citizen scientist. With your help, Edgardo would record where and when you spotted the manta, and local divers would photograph the manta's belly to help identify it. All the information your tour group gathered would be entered into Planeta Océano's manta ray database.

"Before if [a manta ray] got stuck in the net, we'd grab it, stick a knife in it, then tie it onto the boat and take it to the shore," Edgardo says. Fishers would do anything to save their nets. But not anymore. Cutting their nets has become a point of pride with most fishers from the Tumbes region. Edgardo says, "We cut the net. . . . [We] do this knowing that ecotourism will be the future for [fishers]." The ripples of a giant manta ray's tragic death resulted in an amazing partnership that transformed Edgardo from manta hunter to manta ambassador.

LOCKDOWN

Everything was swimming along nicely until the COVID-19 pandemic spread across the globe in 2020.

Connecting Schools on Zoom allowed youth from different countries to share their thoughts about the ocean.

Like most of the world, Perú shut down. Schools closed and tourism ceased—including the manta ray ecotours. Fishers continued to fish with Planeta Océano's guidelines in mind by respecting fish size limits to allow the fish time to reproduce. They also released sea turtles and giant mantas caught in their nets and picked up garbage floating in the water. But without tourists, their tour boats sat idle for nearly two years and fell into disrepair.

Although ecotourism ground to a halt, Kerstin refused to allow the pandemic to derail her. "We needed to have patience and continue doing things step by step," she says. While students learned from home during the pandemic, Planeta Océano reinvented its Connecting Schools program to encourage online marine conservation discussions. Originally launched in 2018, students from the United States, Central America, Ecuador, and Perú shared ocean conservation ideas on Skype during the Peruvian students' computer lab class. Their teachers guided the discussion. During the pandemic, students connected from their homes through Zoom. Planeta Océano shared photos and videos and divided students into breakout rooms to get to know one another better. Narelle, Kerstin's nine-year-old daughter, listened in as her mom led the conversations. She loved hearing about how kids from various parts of the world thought about the ocean. "I made drawings about all these people from around the world and their ideas," she says. "I saw their happiness for learning about the ocean."

Then, in late 2021, the world slowly began to emerge from its cocoon. Planeta Océano won a grant to reactivate many of its programs, including ecotourism. The grant provided money to repair boats, create a new marketing campaign, and reregister the boats with the government so the fishers could continue educating travelers about mantas.

Kerstin remains optimistic about Perú's giant manta rays. But what does the future hold?

NARELLE'S FAVORITE OCEAN GAME: EXTINCTION!

Narelle is an honorary member of the Planeta Océano team. "I often ask Narelle to be my editor when I make games and activities for children," Kerstin says. "She knows what's fun and what isn't." Extinction! is Narelle's favorite game created by her mother. Give it a try!

Narelle (*seated in the center*) plays Extinction! with her mother (*standing on the right*) and a classroom of students.

Goal

To understand how healthy habitats support marine life

Props

- One chair for every person in the group. Set them up as you would for musical chairs.
- Labels for a variety of ecosystem factors, such as zooplankton (food source), oxygen, pollution-free water, ideal water temperature, healthy habitat, and conservation leaders. Attach one label to each chair.
- Music
- Optional: Manta ray masks designed by each player

How to Play

- Players represent healthy manta rays swimming around the ocean.
- Start the music. Players walk around the chairs. When the music stops, each player finds a seat. (The first time through, there is one chair for each player signaling a healthy ocean.)
- Remove one chair labeled with an ecosystem factor that mantas require, such as water temperature. Briefly mention why the component is important to mantas and how it can be affected. For example, climate change could alter water temperature and affect the manta's distribution or its population numbers.
- Start the music again. Players walk around the chairs. When the music stops, one player will not be able to find a chair and is eliminated.
- Repeat the previous two steps until only one chair remains.
- Discuss what has happened to the manta rays' habitat. Discuss extinction. How can we help species thrive by maintaining the various ecosystem factors they need?
- Optional: Choose a different marine animal. Ideas include sea turtles, sharks, and corals. Consider the ecosystem factors your new animal needs to survive. Play the game again.

CHAPTER 4

Living in Balance

Thanks to Kerstin and Planeta Océano, giant manta rays are now part of the Tumbes community's culture and identity.

As Kerstin reflects on her journey, she's proud of Planeta Océano's successes but knows there's more to do.

When she agreed to help Andrea Marshall find the lost manta ray tag in 2011, she had no idea that the community would rally around giant manta rays to protect the ocean. Manta rays became the face of a growing movement of children, teens, fishers, teachers, and community leaders who want to defend ocean resources. "People now get excited about giant manta rays," Kerstin says. "Before people didn't even know that they existed or maybe didn't even care. Now [the mantas] are part of who they are as a culture and identity."

Josué Granda is one of Kerstin's success stories. Josué has known Kerstin since he was three years old. He toddled after his older sisters when they volunteered for the sea turtle project, and he helped paint murals on school walls with messages about how to care for the ocean. "My father used to fish for manta rays," he says. "When we learned about manta rays from Planeta Océano, our point of view changed." The Grandas became manta ambassadors.

Tumbes children and fishers follow in Kerstin's footsteps working to protect giant manta rays to safeguard their sea.

Mariano Cabanillas first learned about Planeta Océano while working on an assembly line in a fish processing factory. "Besides being wonderful people [the team at Planeta Océano] helped me grow as a person," he says. "They made my life better." Mariano completed a master's degree in oceanography and became a research associate for Planeta Océano.

The first teachers to join the Marine Educators Network are now

Kerstin (*right of Tumbes sign*) and Planeta Océano host a fourteen-year reunion for teachers in the Marine Educators Network.

principals and superintendents in their school districts. "As an administrator, I have the power and opportunity to influence marine education," says Luz Agurto. Martin Dioses wrote his master's thesis on marine education and hopes his district adopts his suggestions into the school curriculum.

One former sea turtle volunteer is now the director of a technical institute in Zorritos that offers fishing technology and computer science majors. The institute provides Planeta Océano with classrooms and technology for their meetings with fishers.

GRATITUDE

Kerstin's unusual three-part strategy—science, education, and sustainability—has earned two prestigious international awards: the Rolex Award for Enterprise and the Whitley Award, frequently called the Green Oscar. The cash prizes from the awards helped her expand Planeta Océano's network across ten coastal communities in Perú. "We want people to understand the richness of the place they live and why they should value what they have," says Planeta Océano team member Alfredo Salazar.

The secret to Kerstin's success is her ability to listen. She never claims to have all the answers. "The experts are in the field," she says of the fishers and teachers she's worked with. "I can learn so much more from them than I can teach them." Together they tap into their connectedness to the ocean and their connectedness to one another to realize their potential.

Planeta Océano's story has spread beyond the coast of Perú, and Kerstin smiles to think that her small organization has inspired the conservation world. Communities across the globe have heard about Kerstin's success and have also embraced an inclusive approach to help local people become the stars of their own conservation stories.

At home in Perú, conservation work continues. Because cultural attitudes about fishing have been passed down for generations, Planeta Océano's mission requires constant effort. Attitudes and habits change slowly. Kerstin's daughter, Narelle, has had only basic ocean education in her Lima school. "I'm quite sure I'll learn more," Narelle says. "Hopefully as much as my mother has taught me." Despite the challenges, Kerstin continues to notice positive steps in her community of manta ambassadors. Some of Planeta Océano's first students now teach children about our connections to the sea. Others study the ocean in college. Fishers take pride in ocean conservation and share their love of the sea with their communities.

"We are a small organization, but we are thinking about impacting the region on a large scale," Kerstin says. While she is grateful for each success, she also knows that conservation work is a marathon, not a sprint. "It's impossible to solve an environmental issue or challenge in a day," Kerstin says. "It takes a lot of time, effort, resources, commitment, and perseverance. That's what drives us forward."

> **"We want people to understand the richness of the place they live and why they should value what they have."**
> —Alfredo Salazar

WHAT'S NEW?

Once Perú legally protected giant manta rays, Planeta Océano refocused on the danger of bycatch. "We need science to understand manta behavior," Kerstin says. Fishers and mantas share the ocean, and because

Kerstin can't teach mantas to avoid fishing nets, she wants to help fishers avoid mantas.

In 2018 Planeta Océano partnered with manta scientists from Stanford University in California to attach satellite tags to giant manta rays swimming in the waters off northern Perú. The team discovered that during daylight hours mantas swam near the surface and traveled between the coast of Perú and the Galápagos Islands. At night, their behavior changed. They dove into deep water to feed and resurfaced every few minutes. "We're analyzing our data to put together maps of hot spots, critical areas where mantas are found," Kerstin says.

Then Planeta Océano and the Allen Institute for AI used this data to adapt the EarthRanger app so fishers could easily report mantas at sea. "We are equipping artisanal fishermen with cell phones so that they can . . . report sightings, not only of giant manta rays, but also of other species of marine megafauna such as whale sharks [sea turtles, birds, and marine mammals]," Kerstin says. Ultimately, the app could help fishers avoid these species that accidentally become entangled in their nets. In the future, Kerstin hopes to support protected areas that help conserve manta rays and other marine life.

Planeta Océano team member Alfredo Salazar (*center*) shows fishers how to use the new EarthRanger app to track manta ray sightings.

In addition, Edgardo and his daughter Zulema conducted a new series of surveys for Planeta Océano to highlight the problem of bycatch from the fishers' perspective. Edgardo and Zulema asked fishers several questions about their bycatch experiences: Were their nets ever damaged or lost? Did they ever lose a catch? Were they reimbursed for their loss? Where was the bycatch animal found? What suggestions did they have for reducing bycatch?

Understanding where and when mantas are likely to swim and how fishers are impacted is key. Kerstin believes the data from these projects will help Planeta Océano create an action plan to reduce bycatch in Perú that is fair to both fish and fishers.

Kerstin trained young people to ask fishers about sightings of critically endangered sawfish.

Planeta Océano's community conservation work does not stop at giant manta rays. Kerstin recently expanded their mission to support a manta ray cousin—the sawfish. Scientists were surprised to find one of these supposedly extinct rays in Peruvian waters. Using Kerstin's sea turtle project as a model, the Planeta Océano team recruited university students to patrol Perú's northern coastline and Ecuador's coastline and ask fishers if they had spotted a sawfish. Kerstin and her team drafted guidelines for the legal protection of sawfish, which the Peruvian government readily accepted. Next, Planeta Océano wants to expand sawfish protection across Latin America.

Sawfish find their prey with their sawlike rostrum, which can detect the individual electrical fields that surround all living creatures. This sawfish was found in northern Perú with a green fishing net entangled in its rostrum.

With Kerstin's help, fishers now support giant manta rays with ecotourism.

Kerstin's story continues to unfold, and she encourages *you* to star in your own story. "I invite you to think about how, from your own role in society, you can help identify an environmental challenge to which the ocean or planet Earth is exposed," she says. Whether you make big steps or small, your goal is to develop a meaningful solution. "Imagine the power if each one of us . . . generated that transformative story."

"Don't wait until you're old like me," says Edgardo, who has been fishing since he was seventeen years old. "I was ignorant for fifty years, but I was able to learn about and appreciate marine life. Now I am one of the protectors. It is the most important thing in my life."

Edgardo's son Erik agrees. "I'm leaving behind the shame of fishing these species," he says. "I feel very proud now protecting them."

Kerstin and Planeta Océano changed the hearts and minds of the people of coastal Perú and won support from the government. Because of their efforts, giant manta rays continue to soar through the deep blue, their fins flapping like wings as their diamond-shaped bodies slice through ocean swells.

OCEAN HEROES

Planeta Océano encourages youth to identify environmental challenges in their communities and design projects to study them. Here are a few questions they explored:

How Does Cleaning a Riverbank Help the Ocean?

When Haron was nine years old, he picked up trash along the river beneath an international bridge between Perú and Ecuador. He collected plastic bags and bottles, old CDs, and cardboard before it reached the ocean. To spread awareness that all trash eventually flows to the sea, Haron used the trash to create costumes for a contest and parade. "I didn't know I was polluting when I threw trash on the ground," Haron says. "Kerstin changed my view of everything. She changed my attitude. She empowered me to speak out when I see someone polluting."

Haron Avila

Do Fish Eat Microplastic?

Jeykob and Christofer chose to find out if fish ate the tiny microplastic pieces floating in the ocean. They bought fish at the fish market, dissected them, and used a chemical on the fishes' stomach contents to simulate digestion. The boys looked at the digested material under a microscope.

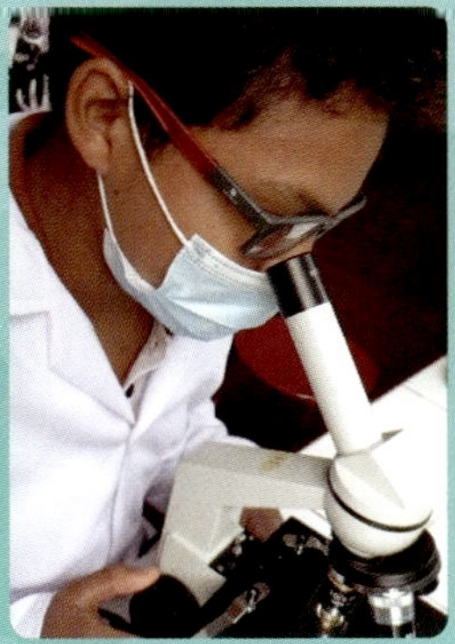

Jeykob García

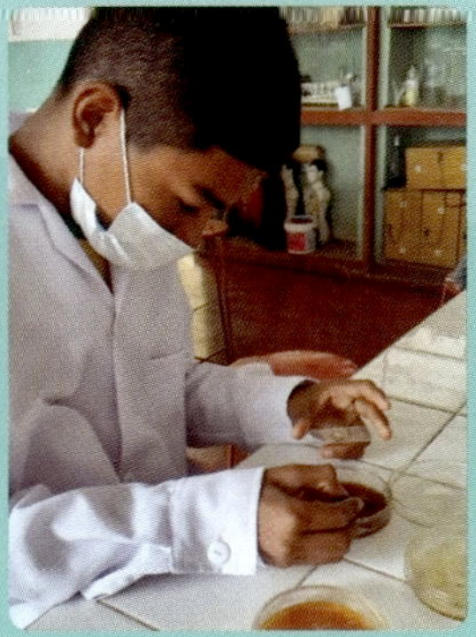

Christofer Ruidias

"The fish eat the microplastic, and we eat the fish!" Christofer says.

"When you find out you're eating plastic, it's sad for humanity," Jeykob says. "We are now more aware about pollution in the sea."

Where Does Our Trash Go?

Dulce discovered that trash from many local farms was tossed in irrigation ditches that washed out to the sea. Camila and Charleny tracked their family's trash to a recycling facility that opened everyone's trash bags and pulled out what they could recycle. Instead of sending the rest of the trash to the dump, the recycling facility was tossing it in the hills where it smelled and attracted insects. The girls organized different community workshops to shed light on these polluting practices and urged the people to ask for changes. Camila and Charleny also shared a skit about their work with kindergarten children. Together they planted ten trees in a new park cleared of trash that the community vowed to protect. "Many people are not aware about how important it is to preserve the sea from contaminants," Charleny says.

Top: Camila Castañeda (*second from left*) and Charleny Saldarriaga (*third from left*)
Bottom: Dulce del Rosario

Kerstin's Path to Success

1985–1991 Kerstin investigates fallen birds' nests, tide pools, and nature books with her parents.

1992 She creates Friends of the School's Zoo.

2002 She starts college to study biology.

2007 Kerstin designs a community sea turtle project.

She graduates from college and starts a new job.

2008 She quits her job to start her own conservation organization.

2009 Kerstin cofounds Planeta Océano and the Marine Educators Network.

2011 She starts working with manta rays.

2015 Kerstin and fisher Edgardo Cruz meet.

Manta ecotourism begins in Perú.

2016 Kerstin wins a Rolex Award for Enterprise for making the world a better place.

2018 She wins the Whitley Fund for Nature Award and Young Global Leader Award.

The Connecting Schools initiative is launched.

2019 *Fortune* magazine includes Kerstin on their World's Greatest Leaders list.

2020 The COVID-19 pandemic begins, and ecotour bookings plummet.

2022 The Connecting Schools initiative evolves in the pandemic.

2023 Kerstin creates a regional strategy to protect critically endangered sawfish and begins to reorganize the ecotours.

Running a nonprofit organization takes constant effort and concentration.

Kerstin accepts her Rolex Award from Sylvia Earle, president and chair of the Sylvia Earle Alliance/Mission Blue and a National Geographic Society Explorer in Residence.

Author's Note

Nonfiction ideas hide in plain sight. Most ideas require some digging to understand my personal connection to them. If I find the connection, the idea becomes a book. If I cannot, I file the idea away. Occasionally, the universe will send me an idea with the connection blinking like a neon sign. As it did for *Giant Rays of Hope.*

I first learned about Kerstin Forsberg in a 2022 *Time* magazine question-and-answer piece, "The Peruvian Marine Biologist on Our Ocean Planet, Working with Fishermen and the Miracle of Manta Rays." Hmmm, it sounded interesting, so I kept reading. The first question Kerstin fielded was "What is the focus of your group Planeta Océano?"

And I stopped. Kerstin named her organization Planet Ocean? I wrote a book called *Planet Ocean!*

So, I took a chance. After some preliminary research, I emailed Kerstin at 4:35 p.m. on May 9, 2022, to ask if I could write her story. Then I held my breath. Would she be interested? Was she too busy to work with me?

By 8:20 p.m. on the same day, I had my answer. "Thank you for your email and interest in our work! I would be delighted to talk with you and explore potential collaboration opportunities," Kerstin wrote.

Over the next year, I interviewed Kerstin, her team, fishers, educators, and children. I planned, then canceled, a research trip to Perú because widespread violence broke out in the country over their president's impeachment. With the help of Zoom and a wonderful translator, we persevered and connected despite Perú's political turmoil.

I hope you enjoyed Kerstin's story. I once heard Michelle Obama describe community service as the work you do for the next generation—it's the rent we pay for living. I like to think of my books as a small contribution towards that rent.

Note from Kerstin

Dear Reader,

Thank you for embarking on this *Giant Rays of Hope* journey with us!

We've reached the end of our book, yet there's still so much more to our story.

We'll keep working hard to avoid mantas from getting entangled, to further protect marine areas and species, and to engage as many people as possible.

On your side, I hope this book helped you recognize that you too can be a changemaker. That you have a powerful voice to share. And that you are never too young to take action.

I now invite you to build on your own story! You can

1. Research the main challenges in your community.
2. Brainstorm ideas on how to help solve one of these issues.
3. Engage friends, family, community members, or local organizations to help you implement your ideas. Any small effort counts. Remember to celebrate your success!

Follow your own path, and please share the message to care for our ocean.

Let's all build a better planet together!

With huge hope for the future,
Kerstin

Acknowledgments

Muchas gracias to the huge number of people who helped make this book a reality. You took me in and made me part of your community. *¡Ustedes son mi inspiración!*

To Kerstin Forsberg and her grand vision for uniting a community, and to her dedicated Planeta Océano staff and volunteers for implementing the vision, including Alfredo Salazar, Laura Barrantes, Mariano Cabanillas, and Ricardo Sanjinez.

To Narelle Casabonne Forsberg for her wisdom about the sea and for sharing her mom with me for so many hours.

To the amazing children and youth who have been forever changed by their work with Planeta Océano, including Ana Tello, Treysi Calderón, Dahja Castañeda, Julio Suárez, Dayra Juarez, Haron Avila, Josué Granda, Camila Castañeda, Christofer Ruidias, Milagros Quispe Espinoza, Dulce del Rosario, Jeykob García, José Zapata, and Charleny Saldarriaga.

To fishers and manta ambassadors Edgardo Cruz and Erik Cruz and to university student and manta ambassador Zulema Cruz for sharing their experiences.

To the teachers of the Marine Educators Network for your passion and commitment to ocean education, including President Yilmer Roque, Jacinto Castillo, Luz Agurto, B. Martin Dioses, Vitalia Brito, and María del Pilar Dios.

To Oscar Gabriel Prieto, archaeologist, University of Florida, and Giannina Bardales, curaduria, Manejo de Colecciones, Museo Larco, for your expertise on the Moche civilization.

To Andrea Marshall whose pioneering work with manta rays helped Kerstin build her program in Perú.

To Kelly Cruz Cumpen and Efren Eduardo Rodriguez Martinez for their photograph of Edgardo's giant manta ray.

To Ernesto Paredes for translating our many interviews from Spanish to English.

To photographers Joost van Uffelen, Corey Rae Neves, and Gisela Kaufman and to the team at the Rolex Awards and Planeta Océano for the beautiful photos.

Glossary

ambassador: an official representative or messenger that speaks on behalf of an idea, group, or animal, such as giant manta rays

artisanal fisher: individual fishing household that fishes close to shore with simple gear and a small boat

bycatch: the accidental capture of marine animals in fishing gear (hooks, nets, traps)

coastline: the boundary between land and sea

conservation: the preservation and protection of something, such as nature

dorsal: the back of an animal

eco-friendly: not harmful to nature

ecotourism: vacationing that minimizes our impact on the environment

entangle: to trap or ensnare

food web: interacting food chains in a habitat

gill plate: a ring of feathery filaments that filter out plankton for giant manta rays

harpoon: a barbed spear usually used in hunting large fish or whales

Humboldt Current: a north-flowing current along the coast of Chile and Perú responsible for the area's high plankton production

Mobula birostris: the scientific name for the oceanic (or giant) manta rays that swim off the coast of Perú and Ecuador

Moche: an ancient civilization that lived near Perú's coast about 100 to 800 C.E.

overfishing: to deplete the stock of fish by too much fishing

phytoplankton: tiny aquatic plants that make about half of the world's oxygen

satellite tracking device: a tool for following the movements of wild animals

upwelling: upward movement of deep, cold, nutrient-rich water to the ocean's surface

ventral: the belly side of a manta ray or other animal

zooplankton: tiny animal life in the sea near the bottom of the food chain

Source Notes

6 Kerstin Forsberg, WhatsApp message to the author, December 28, 2023.

6 Kerstin Forsberg, "La Comunidad que Protegió a las Mantarrayas Gigantes | Kerstin Forsberg | TEDxPaseoYortuque," translated by YouTube's translate feature, YouTube video, 16:41, TEDx Talks, posted July 29, 2020, https://www.youtube.com/watch?v=3G7kX8Wqq7M.

6 Andrea Marshall, interview with the author, November 18, 2022.

6 Kerstin Forsberg, quoted in "Kerstin Forsberg on Changing the Way Marine Conservation Works | Next Generation Leaders | TIME," *Time*, posted May 24, 2018, YouTube video, 3:35, https://www.youtube.com/watch?v=PIAAut3KOeY.

6 Forsberg.

9 Kerstin Forsberg, "Kyosha, la Ballenita de Paz," translated by Google Translate, *Apple Magazine*, 1994, Newton College Lower School, 45.

10 Kerstin Forsberg, interview with the author, January 23, 2023.

11 Kerstin Forsberg, "Kerstin Forsberg, ¡Salvemos la Mantarraya!" translated by YouTube's translate feature, DW Español, posted November 5, 2018, YouTube video, 26:01, https://youtu.be/KwL0G4Vjsy8.

12 Ana Tello, interview with the author, translated by Ernesto Paredes, March 13, 2023.

13 Forsberg, "Kerstin Forsberg, ¡Salvemos la Mantarraya!"

13 Forsberg, "La Comunidad que Protegió a las Mantarrayas Gigantes."

13 Forsberg.

14 Forsberg, interview, January 23, 2023.

14 José Zapata, interview with the author, translated by Ernesto Paredes, March 14, 2023.

15 Milagros Quispe Espinosa, interview with the author, translated by Ernesto Paredes, March 14, 2023.

16 Kerstin Forsberg, quoted in "The Huge Power in Every Woman and Every Little Girl to Transform Ocean Science and Conservation," UNESCO, updated April 20, 2023, https://www.unesco.org/en/articles/huge-power-every-woman-and-every-little-girl-transform-ocean-science-and-conservation.

16 Dayra Juarez, interview with the author, translated by Ernesto Paredes, March 14, 2023.

16 Treysi Calderón, interview with the author, translated by Ernesto Paredes, March 13, 2023.

16 Narelle Casabonne Forsberg, interview with the author, translated by Kerstin Forsberg, February 27, 2023.

16 Dahja Casteñeda, interview with the author, translated by Ernesto Paredes, March 14, 2023.

16 Jeykob García, interview with the author, translated by Ernesto Paredes, March 14, 2023.

17 Julio Suárez, interview with the author, translated by Ernesto Paredes, March 14, 2023.

17 Suárez.

17 Martin Dioses, interview with the author, translated by Ernesto Paredes, February 22, 2023.

19 Kerstin Forsberg, quoted in Franck Sanson, "Kerstin and the Giant Manta Rays," produced by Pronto Prod and Ushuaïa TV, 2017, Vimeo video, 52:05, https://vimeo.com/256771795, password required for viewing.

21 Ricardo Sanjinez, interview with the author, translated by Ernesto Paredes, March 10, 2023.

22 Sanjinez.

23 Gwynn Guilford, "Manta Rays and Human Babies Are the Latest Victims of Traditional Chinese Medicine," Quartz, June 13, 2014, https://qz.com/220326/manta-rays-and-human-babies-are-the-latest-victims-of-traditional-chinese-medicine.

26 Kerstin Forsberg, "Kerstin Forsberg: Manta Ray Conservation in Peru," New England Aquarium, posted November 4, 2016, YouTube video, 58:01, https://www.youtube.com/watch?v=Sxc-9XClzrQ.

27 Forsberg, quoted in Sanson, "Kerstin and the Giant Manta Rays."

27 Forsberg, "Kerstin Forsberg: Manta Ray Conservation in Peru."

27 Forsberg.

31 Erik Cruz, interview with the author, translated by Ernesto Paredes, March 11, 2023.

31 Cruz.

31 Edgardo Cruz, interview with the author, translated by Ernesto Paredes, February 19, 2023.

31 Cruz.

32 Forsberg, "La Comunidad que Protegió a las Mantarrayas Gigantes."

32 Forsberg.

32 Forsberg, "Kerstin Forsberg: Manta Ray Conservation in Peru."

32 Forsberg.

33 Kerstin Forsberg, interview with the author, January 26, 2023.

34 Kerstin Forsberg, quoted in "Kerstin Forsberg Is Fighting for Manta Rays," CNN: Call to Earth, October 17, 2022, https://www.cnn.com/videos/world/2021/06/08/kertsin-forsberg-ocean-spc-intl-c2e.cnn.

34–35 Edgardo Cruz, interview.

34 Forsberg, quoted in "Kerstin Forsberg Is Fighting for Manta Rays."

35 Edgardo Cruz, quoted in "A Biologist Protecting Peru's Giant Manta Rays from Being at Risk," CGTN America, posted on July 8, 2019, YouTube video, 9:09, https://america.cgtn.com/2019/07/08/a-biologist-protecting-perus-giant-manta-rays-from-being-at-risk.

36 Kerstin Forsberg, interview, January 26, 2023.

36 Narelle Casabonne Forsberg, interview.

37 Casabonne Forsberg.

39 Kerstin Forsberg, quoted in "A Biologist Protecting Peru's Giant Manta Rays from Being at Risk," CGTN America.

39 Josué Granda, interview with the author, translated by Ernesto Paredes, March 14, 2023.

39 Mariano Cabanillas, interview with the author, translated by Ernesto Paredes, March 10, 2023.

40 Luz Agurto, interview with the author, translated by Ernesto Paredes, February 22, 2023.

40 Alfredo Salazar, interview with the author, translated by Ernesto Paredes, March 10, 2023.

41 Kerstin Forsberg, interview, January 26, 2023.

41 Salazar, interview.

41 Narelle Casabonne Forsberg, interview.

41 Kerstin Forsberg, WhatsApp message to the author, December 29, 2023.

41 Kerstin Forsberg, quoted in Kate Samuelson, "Fighting to Save Our Oceans," *Time*, May 17, 2018, https://time.com/collection-post/5277968/kerstin-forsberg-next-generation-leaders/.

41 Kerstin Forsberg, interview, January 23, 2023.

42 Forsberg.

42 Kerstin Forsberg, quoted in "La Lucha a Contra Reloj por Salvar a las Mantarrayas Gigantes de Perú," translated by YouTube's translate feature, CNN Español, June 15, 2023, https://cnnespanol.cnn.com/2023/06/15/mantarrayas-gigantes-peru-planeta-oceano-cte-llamado-tierra/.

44 Forsberg, "La Comunidad que Protegió a las Mantarrayas Gigantes."

44 Edgardo Cruz, interview.

44 Erik Cruz, interview.

45 Haron Avila, interview with the author, translated by Ernesto Paredes, March 14, 2023.

45 Christofer Ruidias, interview with the author, translated by Ernesto Paredes, March 14, 2023.

45 García, interview.

45 Charleny Saldarriaga, interview with the author, translated by Ernesto Paredes, March 14, 2023.

Selected Bibliography

"A Biologist Protecting Peru's Giant Manta Rays from Being at Risk." CGTN America, July 8, 2019. https://america.cgtn.com/2019/07/08/a-biologist-protecting-perus-giant-manta-rays-from-being-at-risk.

Avila, Haron, and Josué Granda, youth volunteers. Interviewed by the author, March 14, 2023.

Brito, Vitalia, teacher. Interviewed by the author, March 10, 2023.

Casabonne Forsberg, Narelle, Kerstin's daughter. Interviewed by the author, February 27, 2023.

Castañeda, Camila, Christofer Ruidias, Milagros Quispe Espinoza, Dulce del Rosario, Jeykob García, José Zapata, and Charleny Saldarriaga, high student volunteers. Interviewed by the author, March 14, 2023.

Casteñeda, Dahja, Julio Suárez, and Dayra Juarez, students. Interviewed by the author, March 14, 2023.

Castillo, Jacinto, Luz Agurto, B. Martin Dioses, Yilmer Roque, Vitalia Brito, and María del Pilar Dios, Marine Educators Network. Interviewed by the author, February 22, 2023.

Cruz, Edgardo, fisher and Planeta Océano ambassador, and his daughter Zulema Cruz, university student. Interviewed by the author, February 19, 2023.

Cruz, Erik, fisher. Interviewed by the author, March 11, 2023.

Forsberg, Kerstin, director, Planeta Océano. Interviewed by the author, January 23, January 26, and August 15, 2023.

"Kerstin Forsberg Is Fighting for Manta Rays." Call to Earth. Accessed October 17, 2022. https://www.cnn.com/videos/world/2021/06/08/kertsin-forsberg-ocean-spc-intl-c2e.cnn/video/playlists/call-to-earth/.

New England Aquarium. "Kerstin Forsberg: Manta Ray Conservation in Peru." Posted on November 4, 2016. YouTube video, 58:01. https://youtu.be/Sxc-9XClzrQ.

Salazar, Alfredo, Laura Barrantes, Mariano Cabanillas, and Ricardo Sanjinez, Planeta Océano staff and volunteers. Interviewed by the author, March 10, 2023.

Samuelson, Kate. "Fighting to Save Our Oceans." *Time*, May 17, 2018. https://time.com/collection/next-generation-leaders/5277968/kerstin-forsberg-next-generation-leaders/.

Stevens, Guy, Daniel Fernando, Marc Dando, and Giuseppe Notarbartolo di Sciara. *Guide to the Manta and Devil Rays of the World*. Princeton, NJ: Princeton University Press, 2018.

Tello, Ana, and Treysi Calderón, youth volunteers. Interviewed by the author, March 13, 2023.

Diving Deeper

Books

Cousteau, Philippe, Deborah Hopkinson, and Meilo So. *Follow the Moon Home: A Tale of One Idea, Twenty Kids, and a Hundred Sea Turtles*. San Francisco: Chronicle Books, 2016.
Discover another community project that increased ocean awareness and spotlighted sea turtles.

Kirby, Loll, and Adelina Lirius. *Old Enough to Save the Planet*. New York: Magic Cat, 2021.
Read about twelve children from around the world who are making positive changes in their communities.

Newman, Patricia, and Annie Crawley. *Planet Ocean: Why We All Need a Healthy Ocean*. Minneapolis: Millbrook Press, 2021.
Planet Ocean shows us how to stop thinking of ourselves as existing separate from our ocean and how to start taking better care of this precious resource.

Websites

MantaMatcher
https://mantamatcher.org/gallery.jsp
MantaMatcher allows divers to upload their photos of unique manta ray ventral side patterns. Check out the gallery.

Mission Blue
https://missionblue.org/
Sylvia Earle ignites public support to establish a global network of marine-protected areas called Hope Spots. Learn more about her work and how you can support the Hope Spot closest to you.

New England Aquarium's Marine Conservation Action Fund
https://www.neaq.org/conservation-and-research/marine-conservation-action-fund/
The New England Aquarium is a research center and conservation organization. Visit this website to plan your visit to see its collection of marine animals. The aquarium also regularly supports Planeta Océano in its mission to empower locally led ocean action around the world.

Planeta Océano
https://www.planetaoceano.org/
Visit Planeta Océano's official website to learn more about their programs and meet the people behind the organization's conservation work.

Rolex Perpetual Planet Initiative
https://newsroom.rolex.com/world-of-rolex/perpetual-planet
Learn about Rolex's program to support individuals and organizations that protect the planet.

Index

Photo Acknowledgments

Image Credits: Joost van Uffelen, pp. 4, 7 (left), 18, 20, 44; © Rolex/François Schaer, pp. 5, 11, 13, 21 (right), 22, 26, 31, 35, 37, 39, 45 (top right), 45 (top); Marine Megafauna Foundation, p. 6; Natalia Pryanishnikova/Alamy, p. 7 (middle); Corey R. Nevels, pp. 7 (right), 29, 30, 38; Forsberg family, p. 8; Planeta Océano, pp. 9, 12 (top), 12 (bottom), 36, 43 (right); Tello family, p. 12 (middle); Nicolas Remene/Le Pictorium/Alamy, p. 14 (left); Zapata family, p. 14 (right); Espinoza family, p. 15 (top left); Noemí Pinedo, p. 15 (top left); Suárez family, p. 15 (bottom); Juarez family, p. 16 (top left); Cromo, p. 16 (top right); Calderón family, p. 16 (bottom left); Castañeda family, p. 16 (bottom middle); García family, p. 16 (bottom left); Museo Larco, Lima - Perú, p. 17; Mint Images RF/Getty Images, p. 19 (top); John Giustina/Getty Images, p. 19; Mario Moreno/Getty Images, p. 19 (bottom right); Miguel Gómez, p. 21 (left); Gisela Kaufman, p. 23; Doug Perrine/Alamy, p. 24; Duncan Murrell/Alamy, p. 25 (top); WaterFrame/Alamy, p. 25 (bottom); Julio Socola, pp. 27, 40; Avalon.red/Alamy, p. 28 (bottom); Kelly Cruz Cumpen and Edourdo Rodriguez, p. 32; pcess609/Getty Images, p. 33 (top); Chain45154/Getty Images, p. 33 (bottom); © Rigoberto Rosas-Luis, p. 43 (left); Ávila family, p. 44 (top left); Jeasmire Núñez, p. 45 (bottom left), 45 (bottom right); Martha Silva, p. 45 (middle); © Rolex/Nick Harvey, p. 46 (bottom). Design Element: PatternUniverse.

Front cover: Ken Kiefer 2/Getty Images.